CHANGING
Families

Adoptive Families

Leanne Currie-McGhee

ReferencePoint
Press®

San Diego, CA

About the Author
Leanne Currie-McGhee has been writing educational books for over a decade. She is the proud mom to Grace and Hope, both of whom are adopted from China.

© 2019 ReferencePoint Press, Inc.
Printed in the United States

For more information, contact:
ReferencePoint Press, Inc.
PO Box 27779
San Diego, CA 92198
www.ReferencePointPress.com

LIBRARY OF CONGRESS CATALOGING-IN-PUBLICATION DATA

Name: Currie-McGhee, Leanne, author.
Title: Adoptive Families/by Leanne Currie-McGhee.
Description: San Diego, CA: ReferencePoint Press, Inc., 2019. | Series:
  Changing Families | Includes bibliographical references and index.
Identifiers: LCCN 2017054829 (print) | LCCN 2017057232 (ebook) | ISBN
  9781682823569 (eBook) | ISBN 9781682823552 (hardback)
Subjects: LCSH: Adoption—United States—Juvenile literature. | Adopted
  children—United States—Juvenile literature. | Families—United
  States—Juvenile literature.
Classification: LCC HV875.55 (ebook) | LCC HV875.55 .C87 2019 (print) | DDC
  306.874—dc23
LC record available at https://lccn.loc.gov/2017054829

Contents

Chapter One

How American Families Are Changing

When Curtis and Margaret Rogers married, they had hoped to start a family. And that is what they did, but not in the way they originally planned. After trying unsuccessfully to get pregnant, they decided to adopt. During the process of meeting with adoption agencies and social workers, the Rogerses were asked many questions. One was whether they were open to adopting a child of another race. The Rogerses are both Caucasian. Both said yes. "Once I decided to adopt a child, the race and sex became irrelevant," Curtis writes. "We were asking God and a birthmother for the privilege and blessing of being parents. Personally, I felt closing our hearts to a child of another race would be petty and disingenuous."[1]

A Mostly Typical Life

They eventually adopted two boys, a couple of years apart. Both boys are African American. While their route to parenthood was not the same as most, the Rogerses' lives are like those of most other families. Curtis is retired from the US Air Force and spends his days as a stay-at-home dad caring for their boys. Margaret works outside the home. Daily life is a mix of work, school, sports, and social events—typical of most families.

Despite the normality of their lives, the Rogerses do admit that being an adoptive and biracial family has added challenges that many other families do not encounter. These challenges arose early. Curtis remembers one of the first times the couple took their eldest son out. He was still an infant. Curtis cuddled his son as they waited in line at a deli. An older African American woman approached him and asked if the baby was his son. When he said yes, she asked what qualified him and his wife to raise an African American child. "My wife and I looked at each other. By now, it was pretty clear that our adoption of an African American child had social implications that we didn't consider,"[2] Curtis writes. Through this and other encounters, the Rogerses came to realize that a part of their lives would probably always be devoted to dealing with the cultural and social biases of other people.

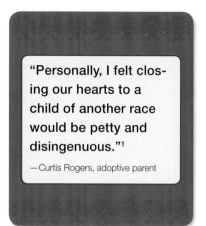

"Personally, I felt closing our hearts to a child of another race would be petty and disingenuous."[1]

—Curtis Rogers, adoptive parent

The Rogerses have not allowed these views to distract them from what they consider to be their primary role. What matters most, Curtis says, is being a good father. In his view, this means addressing adoption and race issues throughout his sons' lives and, at the same time, doing what every father should do. Whether his sons were adopted or not, he says, his ultimate job is to be there for them. After the adoption of their first son, he wrote:

> I am still this child's Daddy. I enforce the rules, give gentle disciplinary reminders, provide support, toss the baseballs, wipe away the tears, kill the spiders, read bed time stories and scare the crocodiles from under the bed. I'm a good Daddy. My wife is a wonderful Mom. We also love our son enough to recognize that sometimes we don't have the answers, and we will do what it takes to figure them out.[3]

Families and Diversity

Families like the Rogerses—with adopted children and children who are a different race from their parents—are much less rare than they once were. Social changes over the past several decades have reshaped American families. These social changes include

US Adoption Trends

Adoptions in the United States have fluctuated over time, with numbers rising fairly consistently from 1951 to a peak in 1970. Since then adoptions show no apparent pattern as they have both risen and fallen, according to the authors of the 2017 study "Adoption: By the Numbers." The study looks at adoption trends between 1951 and 2014.

Year	Total Adoptions	Year	Total Adoptions
1951	72,000	1969	171,000
1955	93,000	1970	175,000
1957	91,000	1971	169,000
1958	96,000	1972	148,701
1959	102,000	1973	148,000
1960	107,000	1974	138,000
1961	114,000	1975	129,000
1962	121,000	1982	141,861
1963	127,000	1986	104,088
1964	135,000	1992	115,689
1965	142,000	1996	108,463
1966	152,000	2002	130,269
1967	158,000	2007	133,737
1968	166,000	2014	110,373

Source: Jo Jones and Paul Placek, "Adoption: By the Numbers," National Council for Adoption, 2017. www.adoptioncouncil.org.

higher divorce rates, more women having children while single or not married to their partner, rising numbers of mothers in the workforce, and increasing numbers of single-parent households. "As a result of these changes," the Pew Research Center writes, "there is no longer one dominant family form in the U.S. Parents today are raising their children against a backdrop of increasingly diverse and, for many, constantly evolving family forms."[4]

Adoption is one way families form. According to a 2017 report by the National Council for Adoption, approximately 110,373 youth were adopted in America in 2014. This equates to about 2 percent to 4 percent of all families having adopted children and results in 2.5 percent of all US children younger than age eighteen being adopted.

Adoption Scenarios Have Changed

Three decades ago, most adoptions in the United States occurred when a young, unmarried woman became pregnant and chose not to keep her baby. Some adoptions still occur this way, but other scenarios are becoming increasingly more common.

Adoptions of young people in foster care are now among the most common adoptions. According to a 2017 National Council for Adoption report, approximately 42 percent of adoptions in 2014 involved youth who were in foster care. Children enter foster care when their parents cannot care for them properly; the cause of this may be neglect, abuse, drug addiction, or incarceration. The goal of foster care is for youth to stay in a stable family until they can be reunited with their biological parents. However, this is not always possible. In cases in which the biological parents do not meet the state's requirements after a certain amount of time, their legal rights as parents are terminated. These children are then available to be adopted.

The children available for adoption from foster care are of a wide age range. Many have experienced traumatic situations before being placed in foster care; some have undergone significant difficulties after being placed there. Many people who adopt foster care youth do so because they realize the need for these children to be in loving families. Caitlin and her husband adopted two of their children from foster care. "We decided together that we would adopt first, before attempting to have biological children," she writes. "It was also important to us that we pursue adoption for kids that were in need of a family, which is why we chose to adopt from foster care vs. domestic infant adoption."[5]

Other adoptions involve children born outside of the United States. International adoptions, in which US citizens adopt from other countries, constitute about 6 percent of total adoptions. Over the years the most receptive countries to US adoptions have been China, South Korea, Russia, and Ethiopia. Many of these countries have large populations of babies and young children whose parents have died or are so poor that they have given them up in hopes that their children will have a better life. International adoptions are increasingly attractive for several reasons. One is the desire to give a home to the many children in need. Other reasons include the fact that domestic adoptions can take a long time, while international adoptions often proceed more quickly. Karen Becker, parent to two children adopted from South Korea, explains:

> The main, short answer, as to why we decided to adopt internationally was that I had had four pregnancies and five babies—one set was twins—but I lost all of them because they were ectopic pregnancies. After losing so many, we really just wanted a sure thing. We had looked into the different types of adoption that were available, and felt international was the surest thing. We really just wanted to have a child like everyone else.[6]

The remainder of adoptions are done through private agencies or set up between private individuals, with a lawyer to facilitate the adoption. These adoptions include infants from young unwed mothers, women in financial crisis, women who are dealing with addiction, or women who, for various reasons, feel incapable of raising a child.

Who Is Adopting?

Who is adopting has also changed over the years. Three decades ago, married childless, heterosexual couples made up the majority of adoptive parents. Today single adults (male and female); married couples with biological children; and lesbian, gay, bisexual, and transgender (LGBT) singles and couples all adopt.

One of the largest group of people who adopt are relatives of the children being adopted. The National Council for Adoption's 2017 report revealed that just over 35 percent of all adoptions involve relatives. For instance, a grandparent, aunt or uncle, or other relative adopts a young family member. This may occur if the biological parent or parents die, lose custody due to maltreatment or neglect, or are incarcerated, among other reasons. These relatives may be single or married, or male or female, LGBT or not—as long as they are able to provide a stable home for the children.

Another reason for the diversity in adoptive parents is the increase in LGBT adoptive parents. This increase has mainly occurred in the past two decades because many states changed laws that prohibited LGBT parents from adopting. Although some agencies still reject LGBT applications, various court rulings have resulted in the legality of adoption by same-sex couples in all fifty states. According to the Williams Institute, a think tank at the University of California–Los Angeles School of Law, more than sixteen

The More the Merrier

Although the American family is changing to include many different types of families, the Sysamek family stands out. Nikki and Michael Sysamek are parents to nine children, five adopted and four biological children ranging in age from seventeen to three. All five of their adopted children are from China and were born with special needs ranging from spina bifida to blood disorders. The Sysameks say that after having four biological children, they felt called to do more and that they had more of themselves to give.

They decided to adopt, and the idea of adopting children with special needs felt right to them. The Sysameks live a daily life that is quite busy—Nikki homeschools the children, they attend numerous medical appointments due to the children's special needs, and they go on frequent shopping trips, since the family drinks a gallon of milk a day. In many ways, it is an unusual life when compared to others' lives, but the Sysameks view the differences as blessings and an adventure. "This is our passion that we just believe the Lord has given to us," says Nikki.

Quoted in Joseph Goodman, "A Day of Football for a Family with Five Adopted Children of Special Needs," AL.com, October 4, 2017. www.al.com.

Three decades ago, married heterosexual couples made up the majority of adoptive parents. Today, there is more diversity among adoptive parents, including LGBT parents.

thousand same-sex couples were raising an estimated twenty-two thousand adopted children in the United States as of 2013—the most recent year for such numbers. Many children adopted by LGBT parents have become vocal about their experiences, in order to promote more adoption. Michael Arden-Sonego, now in his twenties and studying to become a firefighter, recalls:

> When the social worker told me that the couple that wanted to adopt my brothers and me was two men, she waited for some reaction, but I didn't care. I just wanted to live somewhere I could call home, somewhere where I could finally relax and know my brothers and I were going to be taken care of. Besides new parents we got a big family with cousins, grandparents, aunts, uncles and four dogs. My parents are good-hearted people who have worked hard to give us many opportunities and I am very grateful to have them as parents.[7]

Many single adults are also adopting. According to numbers released in June 2016 from the Adoption and Foster Care Analysis and Reporting System, of the nearly 428,000 children in foster care, 53,549 were adopted; 26 percent were adopted by single females and 3 percent by single males. The reasons single men and women adopt are the same as other people's reasons—they want to be parents. Some do not want to wait until they are married to have children. Others do not plan to marry. Adoption provides them a way to become parents. Leah Campbell was single when she developed health issues in her midtwenties that meant she needed to try to become pregnant at that time or never have the option. She went through two failed rounds of in vitro fertilization with a sperm donor and then decided to adopt. At age twenty-nine, she adopted a daughter. "I had always wanted to be a mother. . . . So I decided that I would rather be a single mother than to never be a mother at all,"[8] Campbell explains.

"I had always wanted to be a mother. . . . So I decided that I would rather be a single mother than to never be a mother at all."[8]

—Leah Campbell, single adoptive parent

Different Race

Another change is that there are now more people who are adopting children of a different race or ethnicity from their own. This is due to the fact that race matching, the practice of matching adoptive parents with children of the same race, is no longer the prevailing practice of adoptions. Up until as recently as the 1990s, social service workers attempted to place children in adoptive families that shared the child's racial-ethnic background, and in many places this was the law.

The laws that set the rules for adoption were changed and now do not allow race to be considered in child placement decisions. The reasoning for this change is to increase the number of children adopted and because studies have showed transracial adoptions are not harmful to children and are better than long-term institutional care. As a result, today more than 40 percent of adoptions are transracial in nature, according to a recent survey from the US Department of Health and Human Services.

Jillian Lauren and her husband, Scott Shriner, bassist for the band Weezer, became parents through adoption. They adopted their eldest son in 2009 from Ethiopia, a country in northeastern Africa. Their younger son is African American and was adopted from foster care in 2015. Lauren and Shriner are both Caucasian. They view their mixed-race family as special, but much like other parents, they also rejoice in seeing the many stages of growth in their children. In her blog, Lauren writes, "Truly you are a miracle, my glorious son. You couldn't hold a crayon, and now you write your name. You could barely speak and now you know all your letters. You couldn't count to three and now you count to fifty."[9]

Open Adoptions

The arrangements that bring families together are also not all the same as they once were. For many years closed adoptions were the norm. A closed adoption is when the child and the adoptive parents have no identifying information about the biological parents and absolutely no contact with them. Today closed adoptions are still the norm for international adoptions. And while foster care adoptions are not closed, since adoptive parents know the history of their adopted child, the birth parents cannot legally have contact with their birth children after adoption because their legal rights were terminated. However, domestic private adoptions, which were once almost exclusively closed, are now mostly open in some form.

An open adoption is when adoptive parents and their child have identifying information about the birth parents. In many of these adoptions, the birth parent and adoptive parents meet each other, and often it is the birth parent who actually chooses who will adopt her child. Depending on the agreement made at the time of the adoption, the birth parent's contact with the child might end shortly after the adoption, or it might continue in some fashion. According to a report done by the Evan B. Donaldson Adoption Institute,

The Impossible Happened

At fifteen years old, Crystalanne believed she would never become part of a family. After being relinquished by her mother at age ten, she went through several foster homes and group homes and felt she would always be on her own. Then a couple, Kim and Lori, saw her profile on a foster care adoption site and wanted to meet her. Crystalanne could not believe it, because she had several discipline and behavioral problems, but the couple was adamant that they wanted her to be their daughter. They flew from their home in Texas to Oregon, where Crystalanne lived. Upon meeting, they all felt they were meant to become a family. Kim and Lori adopted Crystalanne on her seventeenth birthday, and she became a part of their family. "Being adopted means not worrying about where I will go next," Crystalanne says. "It means having someone who will help me learn all of the things I don't know yet. It means having hope again."

Quoted in AdoptUSKids, "'Of All the Kids, They Picked Me!,'" October 26, 2015. www.adoptuskids.org.

of forty-four hundred domestic infant adoptions from one hundred agencies, 55 percent were fully open. This means that the adoptive parents and child have ongoing direct contact with the birth parents. In another 40 percent of open adoptions, there is no ongoing direct contact, but the adoptive family and birth parents exchange letters and photos through an intermediary.

A Family

No matter how or why the family came together, and no matter the backgrounds of the children and parents, adoptive families are—first and foremost—families. Rachel Garlinghouse and her husband adopted all three of their children. Like any other family, they are living their daily lives with their own unique challenges and joys. Garlinghouse writes. "My kids are real people. With thoughts and feelings. . . . Our love is real. Our family is real. It's all real."[10]

Chapter Two

How I See Myself and My Family

Adoption can be complicated. People who are adopted experience all sorts of different feelings—about themselves and their families. Some adoptees feel as much a part of their adoptive family as any biological child would. Others feel a distance that they cannot bridge. Some wonder about the life that might have been. Others are content with the life they have. Some think often about their biological parents. Others do not think of them at all. And some people who are adopted experience a mix of these and other feelings. The thing about being adopted is that there is no one way to feel. How adoptees see themselves and their families is as different as each individual involved.

Parents

Many adoptees see their adoptive parents as simply their parents. While they realize there is no biological connection between them, these adoptees view their parents as their own, and they believe their parents see them the same way—as simply their kids. This is how Lisa Cleary sees things. She was adopted when she was an infant. She describes her parents this way: "I use the loose term 'adoptive' parents in that my parents adopted me, but they are just my parents—my real parents, the only ones I have ever known."[11]

Other adoptees see things differently. They might respect but not feel close to their adoptive parents. In some cases the relationship with their parents might be strained and adversarial. One woman who was adopted in the 1960s believes the disconnect she felt with her adoptive parents was due to her unresolved thoughts of her birth family. She writes:

> I always knew I was adopted and it haunted me—perhaps because I had such a bad relationship with my mother, or perhaps because I KNEW something of my birth family. I knew I had [biological] siblings. (I was an only child in my adopted family.) I knew that there were people out there I was connected to but didn't know. I was obsessed with this knowledge and it ate at me.[12]

How Older Kids Feel

Being adopted when older rather than as a baby can also affect a kid's relationship with his or her parents. Often, older adopted youth have clear memories of their biological parents, know why they are being adopted, and have lived with foster families, or in the case of foreign adoptions, they might have lived in an orphanage. These experiences affect their ability to trust and relate to others. For these youth, adoption can initially be traumatic and frightening.

Sara Myerson clearly remembers her adoption and how she felt. She was nine years old and living in a Chinese orphanage when she was told an American family wanted to adopt her. She felt excited and immediately agreed to the adoption. Her new parents flew to China, adopted her, and brought her home. After the initial excitement subsided, Myerson was overcome and confused as she dealt with getting to know new parents and siblings, living in a new country with unfamiliar customs, and not speaking the language. She remembers wanting her new mom to do everything for her. "Even though I was nine and had taken care of myself, I wanted Mom to do things for me, like pick out my clothes," recalls Myerson. They were both frustrated and angry at times. "Instead of getting annoyed when I got mad and said, 'No, you pick,' she should have understood that there were too many choices. I'd taken care of myself too much."[13] Myerson says that this time in her life felt very chaotic. Developing a trusting relationship with her new family took time and was sometimes really hard, but it did happen.

Leslie Tousley also recalls how difficult it was to become a part of a family as an older youth. Her birth father abandoned her birth mother during the pregnancy, and Tousley soon ended up in the foster care system. She lived with several different families until she was nine, when she was adopted. Like Myerson, her feelings were mixed after being adopted. "I longed to be a part of an intact family. I was relieved when I was adopted, but the adjustments didn't end there," Tousley writes. "I was suddenly thrust into being the oldest child and assuming many responsibilities that I was not prepared to handle."[14] She also was expected

Being adopted when older rather than as an infant can affect a child's relationship with their adoptive parents. Older children in a foreign adoption may have lived in an orphanage and had experiences that affect their ability to trust others.

to forget her past, rather than deal with the trauma of the neglect and constant changing of foster families that she experienced up until her adoption. Eventually, Tousley became close with her new brother and sister and with her grandparents, although not with her adoptive parents. Because of her experiences, she continued to fear being abandoned, and that stayed with her even after she was adopted.

Feeling Different

No matter how young people relate to their adopted parents, there are often points in their lives when they feel different because they are adopted. Sometimes it is because of how their parents relate to them. Maria Williams was adopted at age seven by the foster parents with whom she had lived since the age of sixteen months. She never felt like she fit in with her adoptive family. Williams's adoptive mother often made negative comments about her biological mother, and she always introduced her as her "adopted" daughter. Her mother was never satisfied with Williams's grades, looks, or attitude. Also, her mother was not truthful with Maria about her birth family and did not let her know she had biological siblings, as Williams discovered later. Williams developed feelings of resentment and anger toward her adoptive parents. After she discovered the lies she had been told about her birth family, Williams said, "I felt like I had been betrayed in a way that I could not explain or even dream of. I moved out of my parents' home shortly after that. There was just too much stress and something had to give."[15] Williams never felt completely part of her family.

Mae Claire also never felt herself to be fully part of her adoptive family. She is from the French-speaking Caribbean island nation of Haiti. She was adopted at age three by an American family. Her new parents and siblings (the couple's biological children) are Caucasian, and Claire is black. Once in the United States, Claire dealt with the confusion of learning a new language and culture as well as adapting to a new family. She recalls not ever really feeling like she fit in. Her parents contributed to this by treating her differently than their biological children. "As a teenager I struggled a lot because I was not afforded everything my siblings were. The biological children definitely had first choice and their voices were heard—all the time. I was expected to be silent, thankful and grateful."[16] Claire grew up feeling that she was held to a higher standard than her siblings and had to prove her worth for acceptance, leaving her feeling hurt and judged.

Many other adopted youth feel that their parents view them and love them as much as any biological child, but there are times the knowledge that they are adopted strikes unexpectedly. This can happen when they look at a family photo and see the differences. Many adoptees long to look like someone in their family. Whether it is obvious, as in the case of transracial adoptions, or not, adoptees know they do not physically resemble others in their family. This can affect how they feel about themselves and how they feel they are viewed by others. Even those who feel completely a part of their family may experience this. "No one in my family treats me any differently just because I look different," writes Emma Goddard, who is Asian and was adopted from Indonesia by Caucasian parents from America. "Only when I'm out in public am I ever reminded that, 'One of these things is not like the others.'"[17] The outward differences of adoptees and their families remind adopted youth that that they are not biologically related, and no matter how much love they receive from their parents, those differences do not go away.

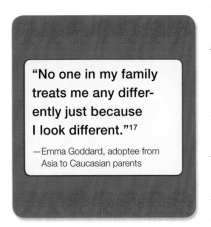

"No one in my family treats me any differently just because I look different."[17]

—Emma Goddard, adoptee from Asia to Caucasian parents

Sense of Loss

The realization that one is different from the rest of one's family sometimes leads to a sense of loss. No matter how joyful an

Not Knowing

Today it is common to tell children at an early age that they are adopted, but that was not always the case. In the past many people who were not told of their adoption discovered the truth much later. Lynne Miller never suspected she was adopted. And then one day she got a call from her sister, who had just made a startling discovery: Both of them were adopted. "I was stunned," she writes. "I felt betrayed by my parents who never so much as hinted at the possibility that I was not their biological daughter. They fooled me and now I felt foolish. Here I was, married, a mother, 38 years old and finding out for the first time that I had been adopted."

By this time, both of Miller's adoptive parents were deceased, so she could not ask them any questions about the circumstances of her adoption and why they kept it a secret. From relatives she learned that she and her sister had been adopted after their parents' biological son had died. Miller felt lost and betrayed. After years of searching, she found her birth parents, and they answered her questions about why she was adopted and who her biological family was. This has helped her achieve more peace in life, but she believes knowing about her adoption early in life would have left her with far less pain and fewer questions.

Lynne Miller, "You're Adopted: The Moment of Truth," Revelations, November 22, 2015. http://lynneamiller.com.

adoption is, it began with some sort of difficulty—or tragedy. Adopted youth know that, whatever the reason, their birth parents gave them up to the care of others. Even those who feel loved and accepted by their adoptive parents sometimes experience a sensation of something missing in their lives. Even though many adoptees have no memory of their birth parents, the longing to know them, or at least know about them, is common.

Ordinary activities, even something as mundane as a routine doctor visit, can trigger feelings of loss. At the doctor's office, patients are asked for their medical history, but some adoptees have no medical history for their biological family. Not being able to answer simple questions about whether there is diabetes or heart

As they grow up, adopted youth have different ways of dealing with complicated feelings involving acceptance and fitting in. However, many do come to realize that the people they share their lives with are their family.

disease in their family can be a frustrating experience. At school, family history projects like making a family tree cause some adoptees stress because of the missing knowledge about their past. Family-tree projects are usually assigned from kindergarten to fourth grade, and often adopted kids are not sure what to do or how to react to these projects. Ruby Cheresnowsky, age ten, was adopted from Guatemala and has issues with these assignments. She says, "They should keep in mind that some adopted kids don't know their [birth] family, and try to come up with ways that they can do their project without having to feel bad that they don't know their family."[18]

Being able to express these feelings of loss is important. Without that outlet, frustration can grow. But sometimes adoptive parents do not know how to deal with the child's feelings; some might encourage their kids to put it in the past and not think about it. This usually makes a young person feel guilt on top of loss. "Growing up, no one ever told me it was okay to be sad about the biggest loss of my life, let alone cry about wanting to know who my birth mother was," writes Pamela Karanova. "Emotions, and sad feelings were tucked deep inside, with no way to come out."[19] Karanova felt guilty about feeling sadness about her biological parents. Not being allowed to express her loss made it more difficult for Karanova to come to terms with being adopted. It was not until she was an adult and decided to search for her birth parents that she began to feel whole.

New Siblings

For most kids, a new sibling can be a real adjustment. For kids who gain new siblings through adoption, the adjustment can bring additional challenges.

Jenna Hardy and her husband have four children: Their two oldest (Sawyer and Chloe) are biological. Their two youngest (Cooper and Piper) are adopted. Each child has a different perspective on becoming siblings through adoption. Sawyer writes that his parents' adoption of his brother and youngest sister is the best thing that ever happened to him. He says he bonded with Cooper immediately. That did not happen with Piper. "She didn't feel like my sister to me once she got home," says Sawyer. And then a few months after she arrived, Piper just suddenly felt like she was his sister.

Cooper, now ten, was three years old when he was adopted from China, and he does not remember much about getting to know Sawyer and Chloe. He just remembers always thinking of them as his brother and sister. But at age nine he gained a new sister when his parents again adopted a child from China. The hard part of gaining a new sibling, he says, was having to adjust to sharing toys—and seeing all of the attention the new child gets. However, the good part of getting a new sibling through adoption, says Cooper, is that he likes having someone who has gone through the same experiences. He told his mother, "She was adopted like me, so when she gets bigger we can talk about that."

Quoted in Jenna Hardy, "Adoption: Through Siblings' Perspectives," No Hands but Ours, December 12, 2017. www.nohandsbutours.com.

Acceptance

Adopted youth have different ways of dealing with what can be a complicated mix of feelings. Some realize and come to accept that there is a part of their lives they will never know. Growing up, Gerald Wozek was bothered by the birthmark on his stomach; it represented a hereditary link to a family and a past he did not know. But over the years he started to realize that the people with whom he shared his life day in and day out *are* his family. "I have met my real brother and real sister and my real mother and my real father in the most uncommon of all places," Wozek writes. "No, this chosen family does not share my bloodline or my experiences of childhood or even my eye-catching birthmark. But my family is as authentic and as genuine as any biological family that I know."[20]

Others, even those who have lived happy childhoods with their adoptive parents, feel the need to search for answers about their birth. For Kelley Marie, searching for her birth parents helped her deal with unresolved feelings about them. She grew up in a family that allowed her to feel free about asking about her birth parents, and her adoptive parents provided her all the information they could. When Kelley Marie became an adult, they helped her search for her biological parents. This journey helped her gain more peace about who she is. Ultimately, it helped her realize how she feels about her adoptive parents. When asked what adoption means to her, she writes, "The feeling I feel most is love. I know that in my life I am loved. I was loved enough by a woman who knew the life she couldn't provide, someone else could. I am loved by my family. I was a miracle; my adoption is a miracle."[21]

"I am loved by my family. I was a miracle; my adoption is a miracle."[21]

—Kelley Marie, adoptee

Chapter Three

How the World Sees Me and My Family

When it comes to the outside world, being adopted can sometimes be an exercise in patience. It is not uncommon for adoptees to be asked questions—lots of questions—about themselves, their adoptive parents, their birth parents, the circumstances of their adoption, and more. Some common questions are: "Are those your real parents?" "Why did your birth parents give you up?" "Did your parents pay a lot to adopt you?" While people who ask such questions are usually just curious about adoption, some questions feel really intrusive. The questions are a constant reminder that the outside world does not fully understand adoption and sees adoptees and their families as different from other families. At times, these views are filtered through hurtful stereotypes. No matter how comfortable an adoptee is with his or her family, the questions and opinions expressed by people outside the family can be trying.

Real Families

"What happened to your 'real' parents?" or some variation on that theme is probably the most common question asked of young people who are adopted. While this question is often not meant in a negative way, to many adoptees it implies that others consider being adopted as something less than real. It suggests that others do not see their family relationships as binding as being related by blood.

The questions about one's real parents often come early, as kids are curious about anything different from their own experiences.

Modern Family Changes Adoption Stereotypes

Historically, adoption was portrayed inaccurately and often negatively in entertainment. Today television shows and movies are becoming more sensitive to adoption. The television show *Modern Family* is considered by many in adoption circles to have been a major part of this shift. In *Modern Family* a gay couple adopts a Vietnamese infant. Despite the show being a sitcom, it depicts realistic situations that adoptive families of today encounter, such as dealing with family reactions and questions from others. Adoptions of Wisconsin, an adoption agency, explains:

> Instead of portraying families created through adoption as "unusual" or "not real" we need to, and have begun to, show the reality of love, thoughtfulness and "normalness" that is adoption. The *Modern Family* Effect bodes well for this change. Sit-coms have always been on the leading edge of how our changing society is portrayed on television, so an accurate and caring portrayal of adoption is a great indicator that adoption will be more fairly and accurately shown in the future.

> Doing so affects how the world views adoption and promotes more understanding and acceptance.

Adoptions of Wisconsin, "The *Modern Family* Effect: Adoption in the Media," 2018. https://adoptionsofwisconsin.com.

When Kembe, who is adopted, was young, he encountered children at the park who incessantly asked him questions about his family. His mother, Kristen Howerton, overheard them saying there is no way she could be his real mother and asking where his real parents are. "I don't think these kids were trying to be cruel," she remembers. "But the way they were surrounding him, asking him questions and refusing to accept his answer as he repeatedly pointed to me as his mom, made the situation feel confrontational."[22] She remarked that her son normally carried himself with confidence, but the questioning and comments intimidated him, and he looked helpless.

The questions about their family relationships never seem to end, according to many adoptees. Dot Saiz, adopted at age two, has encountered numerous adoption questions and comments throughout her life. When she was young, she says, some of the questions even made her cry. As she got older, she realized that most people were not judgmental about adoption, but their questions often seemed rude, even if they did not have ill intent. The questions she has been asked most often are whether she misses her real parents and why she was given up for adoption. She writes that these are personal questions that most adoptees do not want to talk about unless they bring it up. Even though she tires of the questions, Saiz finds herself often explaining the difference between birth parent and "real" parent to others because she wants people to understand.

"There's a HUGE difference between being a 'real' parent and a birth parent," Saiz writes. "My adoptive parents ARE my real parents, and I am thankful for the sacrifice my birth mother made for my well-being."[23]

Even kids who have strong family relationships sometimes start to doubt themselves and their family ties when faced with such personal questions again and again. Julie Fraga was adopted at three months old. Growing up, she was often asked about her birth parents and whether she was going to search for them. These questions trig-gered all sorts of conflicting emotions. "These remarks often felt confusing and hurtful," writes Fraga. "They conveyed an unknow-ing message that it was not 'okay' to simply not know about my biological lineage, and left me feeling exposed for something over which I had no control."[24]

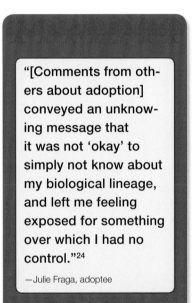

"[Comments from others about adoption] conveyed an unknowing message that it was not 'okay' to simply not know about my biological lineage, and left me feeling exposed for something over which I had no control."[24]

—Julie Fraga, adoptee

Noticeable Differences

In addition to questions from others, looks and comments from others can cause negative feelings in adoptees. Adolescents, in general, like to fit in. They do not like to be seen as different. They do not want to stand out. A kid who is adopted by a family of a different race or ethnicity is most likely going to stand out. Some kids (and some families) deal with this better than others. But even kids who have solid relationships with their parents do not much like the inevitable stares and comments from others.

Emma Goddard is Asian by birth. Her family members are Caucasian. Goddard has a good relationship with her parents and siblings, but sometimes she wishes she looked like them because of how other people see her family. Sometimes when she

Kids like to fit in and do not like to be seen as different. A child who is adopted by a family of a different race is most likely going to stand out to peers.

is out with her father, people ask if they are a couple. The same thing has happened when she is out with her brother. "There are times when I wish I had their fair skin, brown hair, and green eyes just to avoid the stares that I sometimes receive when I'm eating dinner out or I'm at the mall shopping," writes Goddard. "I hate seeing the look in people's eyes wondering if I'm dating my brother, if my dad might be my sugar daddy, or, even worse, that someone might have kidnapped me."[25]

Being treated differently from other family members can also be disconcerting—and confusing. This can happen under the most ordinary of circumstances. Chad Goller-Sojourner has experienced this and does not like the way it feels. He is African American and was adopted at age thirteen by a white couple. As a child, he remembers experiencing racism before he understood what racism actually was. He noticed, for instance, that store employees treated him differently when he was out with his white mother than when he was shopping alone. If the store associates thought he was alone, they would follow him throughout the store. As he got older he encountered a more direct form of racism, including people calling him derogatory names. What was most confusing about this, he says, is that the people calling him these names resembled his parents. "My parents looked like the same people calling me a nigger or porch monkey," Goller-Sojourner recalls. "My mother and my parents were in my corner, but it was still difficult to process."[26]

Young people who are adopted by same-sex couples also have to endure the stares and comments of outsiders. Sarah Gogin was adopted by a gay couple in California in 1988—one of the first such adoptions in that state. She describes growing up in a loving family and remembers weekly pizza and movie nights and parents who were active in her life as assistant soccer coaches and members of school organizations. She also remembers the difficulty of dealing with other people's reactions to her having two fathers. "As I got into grammar school, I didn't understand why people would be treating us differently. You hear things on the playground;" she says, "they throw out these words . . . sometimes without even knowing what it means."[27] Gogin says her parents taught her to deal with these issues head on. Although the prejudice she encountered toward her fathers and her family was hurtful, it also made her strong.

Problem Children

Even when adopted youth and their families do not look any different from other families, adopted adolescents may still be treated differently. Over 40 percent of adopted youth are from foster care, and these youngsters may also be viewed negatively when people discover their background. Some people have developed a negative view of foster care children and believe they are likely to act out or create problems.

Kids in foster care are there because of other people's actions—not their own—but that does not stop people from making assumptions about them. While youth adopted from foster care might need extra help dealing with trauma that occurred earlier in their lives, they are just like other youth. They do not want to be viewed as problem kids, yet many experience a stigma associated with having been in foster care.

> "As I got into grammar school, I didn't understand why people would be treating us differently."[27]
>
> —Sarah Gogin, adoptee, on how others treated her because her parents were gay

Michelle was ten years old when she entered foster care. She was adopted at age sixteen by the foster family she had lived with for three years. This was against the odds, since most foster care children who are adopted are not yet teens. "I think even more than foster parents get a bad rap, foster kids do," Michelle writes. "People seem to think that they, or we, I suppose, are 'troubled,' or just plain trouble. And in a lot of cases, the kids are very troubled—but can you blame them? They need a home where they'll receive the love

Extended Family Viewpoints

Imagine having a grandparent who does not truly view you as her grandchild. Growing up, many adopted youth deal with stereotypes, at times negative, from society. Unfortunately for some, society may include their own extended family. It is extremely hurtful when a person's own family cannot accept him or her. An anonymous writer to *Adoptive Families* magazine does not like the way her own mother treats her three children differently, favoring Troy, her biological child. "My mother recently took her first trip out of the country," the woman writes. "Without telling me, she left a note under Troy's pillow, telling him how much she was going to miss him. She left nothing for my other two children. I found the note and threw it out."

Quoted in *Adoptive Families*, "When Relatives Never Get Adoption." www.adoptivefamilies.com.

and support they need to work through everything that's happened to them."[28] Michelle says that her adoptive parents originally took her in as a foster child because they wanted to help a troubled youth, but then they fell in love with her. She felt the same, and becoming their child provided her a loving family.

The Entertainment Industry's Portrayal

How television shows and movies portray adoption also affects how society views adopted youth and their families. Many shows have reinforced stereotypes about adoption—showing adopted children as more likely to cause trouble or have problems. In the movie *The Avengers*, Thor is told by Black Widow that Loki, his brother, has killed eighty people, and he responds, in a deadpan manner, "Loki is adopted." Jessica Crowell, an adoptee, could not believe it when she heard these lines in the movie and the laughter that resulted. "As an adoptee and comic book fan, I sat in the dark theater stunned," Crowell writes. "I thought of the 12- and

13-year-olds whom I had just seen file into the theater with their parents. Were any of them adopted children as well? Were any of the adults, like me, a member of an adoptive family?"[29]

Other movies imply that adoption does not create the same bond as a biological relationship. In the movie *The Royal Tenenbaums*, the brother and sister (who are adults) realize that she was adopted, then decide it is fine to be attracted to each other. Carrie Goldman, who is adopted and has several brothers and sisters who are also adopted, writes:

> When [the writer] made the two main characters in *The Royal Tenenbaums* fall in love, and it was supposedly okay because Margo was adopted, I was sick to my stomach. By doing this, it was implied that being a brother and sister by adoption does not create the same bond as biological ones, so it is not at all a problem to fall in love with one another. What I want people to know is that we aren't any different from you. My siblings are just that—my siblings. I don't think of them as anything else.[30]

In recent years, television and movies have included more realistic portrayals of adoption. In the television drama *This Is Us*, for instance, the character Randall is a black man who was adopted as an infant by a white family. Randall decides to seek out his birth parents. At one point in the story, he reunites with his birth father. The scene shows Randall experiencing a range of feelings that includes anger at his biological father for abandoning him but also a longing to become closer to him.

From the Outside Looking In

Many young people who have been adopted into loving families appreciate their families. But this feeling might be just one of a complex mix of emotions. They might love their parents

Youth who are adopted from foster care may need extra help dealing with trauma from earlier in their lives. While these children just want to be like other youth, some are viewed as problem kids because of the stigma associated with foster care.

and be happy within their family, while at the same time feeling sadness for the loss of their history and not knowing their birth parents.

One of the more challenging viewpoints for adoptees to handle is that they should be grateful for being adopted. Adoptees often hear people praise their parents for doing a good deed by adopting them and are told that they were lucky to be adopted. When presented with this view, adoptees feel that it does not acknowledge how their lives began and the loss that will never leave them. Mei Webb was adopted at three years old after living in an orphanage for the first years of her life. She loves her parents and is happy with her life and family, but she gets frustrated when people tell her she is lucky. To Webb, this shows a lack of understanding of what adoption means. She explains that not knowing her birth history and having been an orphan is something that will always be a part of her. Webb writes:

> This unluckiness is intangible and will never be fulfilled. It's like a little hole in my heart, very deep and hidden, but still there, that can never be filled. And do you know what? I am OK with that. But please, never tell me I am so lucky (to be adopted), because even though I am lucky to have these second chances and basically everything I could ever want/need, I will never have closure.[31]

Dealing with outside views of adoption, whether positive or negative, can be challenging. The questions, looks, and comments of others often result in emotions ranging from annoyance to sadness. Ultimately, adopted youth just want the world to see their family as any other family that goes through similar good times and bad times.

Chapter Four

Searching for Birth Parents

Cynthia Kortman Westphal enjoyed a happy childhood with a family that she loves. She knew she was adopted, but until she turned ten, she did not think about this fact often. At ten, however, her mind turned to her birth parents after her parents shared with her a file about her adoption. The file contained limited information about her birth parents; it told her their heights, for example, and a little about their ancestry. That was not much, but it was enough to start Westphal thinking about them and wondering what they were like.

Westphal realized she wanted to know more about the woman who gave birth to her and gave her a new life with a new family. Over the years, she tried to find out more, but her search came up empty. Then when she was thirty, the Michigan adoption agency that had handled her case all those years ago informed her that a new state law allowed the agency to share with her the name she was given at birth. That name was Kristen. It was a small piece of information, but it spurred her to resume her search. She discovered she had the right to petition the court that handled her adoption to assign her a mediator who would be able to put her in touch with her birth mother—if the birth mother agreed.

Westphal's birth mother did agree, and the two women e-mailed back and forth for several months before both were ready to meet. That first meeting was emotional. "We laughed and cried so much. We had a good time, but it was weird," Westphal recalls. "All we wanted to do was study each other's faces, but we were so scared. It took a long time before we could even really look at each other, and we're still navigating that, honestly."[32] Westphal says that it took a while to develop a relationship, but they did. Doing so has been satisfying to her; it has answered the questions she has been carrying around with her for a long time.

Like Westphal, many adoptees think about searching for their birth parents. Not all go through with this search. But those who do so find many more avenues open to them now than ever before. Laws in many states have become less restrictive concerning adoptees getting birth information. Plus, as in all aspects of daily life, the Internet has greatly improved the ability to search for anyone and anything.

Mixed Results

Successfully finding one's birth parents does not always end up being emotionally satisfying. For Westphal, it answered many questions and brought a new relationship to her life. Other adoptees have had different experiences.

Lisa Lutz never felt a strong bond to her adoptive parents, did not enjoy a happy childhood, and longed to meet her biological parents someday. She began her search at age twenty-five. Within a short time she obtained the name of her birth mother and contacted her. Her birth mother's reaction was not what she expected. The woman was angry; she had not wanted to be found. Although the two women eventually talked to each other and afterward exchanged letters, Lutz's birth mother ended their contact. Lutz also identified and found her biological father. He seemed pleased to meet her, but after one visit, he did not contact her again or respond to her efforts to stay in touch. Lutz was disappointed with both meetings.

Often, the difficulty with such reunions is expectations. Adam had spent years dreaming about meeting his birth mother. When he finally did, he was excited to see the physical resemblance between them and meet someone he was biologically related to. But then the relationship soured, because she was expecting a close relationship, while Adam was mainly looking for answers and closure. "She had no more children, and a difficult marriage, and wanted more from me than I could give,"[33] Adam recalls.

Whether or Not to Search

At some point in their lives, many adoptees consider searching for their birth parents to answer the questions they have asked themselves and been asked by others for years. Many long to know why their birth parents gave them up. Others just want basic background, such as medical history. Mariah Mills always wondered what her birth parents looked like. She especially thought about them on her birthday, because she knew they were likely thinking of her on that day. She decided to seek out her birth parents in hopes of learning more about her origins. "I've always

Successfully finding one's birth parents does not always end up being emotionally satisfying. Some birth parents react negatively to being contacted and do not wish to have a relationship with the child.

known I was adopted," Mills states. "My mom and dad explained that although my birth parents really loved me, they hadn't been ready to take care of a baby. I had a happy, 'normal' childhood with a loving family, but a huge question mark remained."[34]

Not every adoptee wants to find his or her birth parents. Some choose not to because they worry about hurting their adoptive parents. Others do not want to risk rejection from birth parents a second time. Still others simply do not feel the desire or need to embark on this search. Rosie Garland is in the latter group. She grew up in a loving, happy family. She knew she was adopted; her parents had told her this at a young age. She always felt at peace with herself and her adoption, although like most adoptees, she sometimes wondered about her past. In her thirties she decided to seek out her original birth certificate, just to know her basic birth facts. But when she received it, she decided not to seek out the birth parents listed on the certificate. "I have never felt the need for another family because I have one, with all its loveliness

DNA Matching

At age seventy-four, Carolyn Pooler of Kansas City finally located a biological relative. Pooler, who was adopted as an infant, had spent a lifetime searching for a family connection. She finally located a biological relative through a DNA registry. A DNA registry is a database of DNA profiles. It can be used to analyze genetic diseases, genetic evidence at crime scenes, and genetic connections between family members. A person who wishes to find a biological relative can submit his or her DNA (usually taken from a swab of the inner cheek) and then obtain a list of anyone else in the registry who appears to be biologically related.

After submitting her DNA to the registry, Pooler was contacted by a man who had done the same thing and then discovered they were a match. That man turned out to be her nephew. As the use of registries becomes more common, the chances of adoptees finding biological relatives will also grow.

and angst," Garland writes. "This underpins much of my decision not to search for my family of origin. I've no idea if my birth mother ever told any later partner and children about me. What if I was her big secret? The last thing I would want to do is explode into a stranger's life for selfish reasons."[35]

Difficulties of Searching

Finding one's birth parents is a lot easier than it once was. That does not mean that all such searches succeed. In the case of closed adoptions, such searches can be difficult. Most states allow adoptees age eighteen years or older to obtain nonidentifying information, such as their own date of birth, the age of their birth parents at the time of the birth, the birth parents' religion, and physical characteristics such as race and eye color. About half of the states have instituted laws that allow adoptees to obtain a copy of their original birth certificate, which includes birth parent names. Other states keep the records sealed even after the adoptee is of age. In these cases, adoptees find other ways to carry out their search. Some register with an online adoption database, where birth parents and adoptees list their names and contact info in hopes of finding each other. Others write letters to their state governments asking authorities to release information about them to their birth parents. This is done in the event that birth parents someday contact the state government in an attempt to find their birth child.

"I have never felt the need for another family because I have one, with all its loveliness and angst."[35]

—Rosie Garland, adult adoptee

Stephen Betchen lived in a state that did not provide much information to adult adoptees. In his forties he decided to search for his birth parents but realized he would need help obtaining even the most basic information. With the help of a private investigator, the process went quickly. "The search process, as it is affectionately known, was not for the faint of heart—but it was fascinating," says Betchen. "By calling in a few favors and hiring a private investigator, I was able to have bio mom tracked down within a few days."[36] Betchen adds that the ability to search online has made a huge difference, even when someone starts with little information.

International Searches

For youth adopted from other countries, the search for birth records can be even more difficult. Some countries simply do not have those records—or if they do, they do not make them available. Children who are born in China and adopted by US couples, for example, rarely have access to birth records of any kind. Most were abandoned by their parents—left outside police stations, hospitals, or orphanages with no identifying information. Other countries, such as South Korea, keep records of children who are available for adoption, many of whom were relinquished by an unmarried mother who lacked the means to raise her child. But record keeping is not standardized, and some orphanages and agencies have more detailed and accurate records than others.

Typically, adoptees have the best luck searching if they start with the adoption agency that facilitated their adoption. These agencies have contacts with the countries of adoption. They also have staff who speak the language of the country and can attempt to discover whether there are records and what the laws regarding release of the records are.

Layne Fostervold was born in South Korea and adopted by an American couple in 1973, when he was two years old. Growing up in Minnesota, he was happy with his family but often thought about his birth parents and wanted to know more about them. In 2012 he flew to South Korea and visited the agency that handled his adoption. The social worker was able to show him his adoption file. It showed that his birth mother had contacted the agency in the late 1990s, attempting to find information on him, but the agency did not release any to her. With the contact information she left, Fostervold was able to find her. Although the bonding process between them took a while, in the time since they were first reunited, they have established a close relationship.

What They Learned

For those who reunite with birth parents, the outcomes are varied. For some, it helps them feel whole, and they may even develop an ongoing relationship. Others experience disappointment upon meeting their birth parents. And some who embark on this search do not even get that far; in some cases the birth parents do not want to meet their birth children. This happened to Maggie Geimer.

Geimer was raised by two loving parents, who talked to her about her adoption throughout her life and supported her when she decided to search for her birth mother. At age twenty-one, she was able to obtain her original birth certificate. It included her birth mother's name but no name for her birth father. Rather than attempting to contact her birth mother directly, Geimer asked the agency that oversaw her adoption to make that initial contact. The response was disappointing. The birth mother did not want to meet her. She was only willing to provide a medical history and a few other details of her life. Geimer felt angry and rejected. Eventually, she was able to accept the rejection and felt more at peace with her life. "I don't regret searching my birthmother out. It was a mystery that was looming over my life that is gone

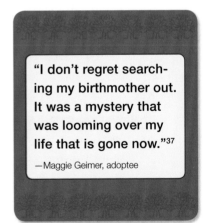

"I don't regret searching my birthmother out. It was a mystery that was looming over my life that is gone now."[37]

—Maggie Geimer, adoptee

now," Geimer says. "Every once in a while, I look at her Facebook profile, not because I'm angry or because I long for a relationship with her, but because we will always be connected. I truly hope she is happy."[37]

Adoptive parents react differently to their adopted child's desire to contact their birth parents. Some are supportive and even help with the search, while others are hurt by the child's need to meet their birth parents.

Reunions between adoptees and birth parents are rarely as dramatic or emotional as fictional portrayals in which the two parties feel an immediate connection, lots of tears flow, and happiness is boundless. What these reunions mostly do is provide answers to long-standing questions and a sense of being able to move forward. This was Kimberly Eddy's experience. She chose not to search for her birth parents until after the birth of her first child. She mainly wanted to find out her medical history and get answers to a few basic questions. "My reunion with each of my biological parents was not of the Hollywood variety," Eddy states. "However, I was able to finally silence the questions that had swirled in my mind for most of my life."[38]

Effects on Adoptive Family

Those who seek out their birth parents find that the search affects their relationships with their adoptive parents in different ways. Some adoptive parents are accepting and even help their children with their search. Others have mixed feelings. They might understand their child's reason for searching but still find it difficult to accept. Others are hurt by their child's need to seek out his or her biological parents, and it causes friction in their relationship.

Eddy might have started looking earlier for her biological mother if her adoptive mother had not seemed so hurt by this idea. Instead, she waited until she was grown and living on her own. And even then she did not share information about her search with her mother until she had located her biological parents. "Because this topic was especially painful for my mother, we chose not to talk about it with her until after we had a successful search," Eddy says. "Though I knew my search had nothing to do with her, my mother felt that any desire I had to find my birth mother was an indictment against her mothering, and I didn't want her to feel that way."[39]

Other adoptive parents are more supportive of their children's searches. Benjamin Hauser, adopted from South Korea by American parents, not only decided to search for his birth parents but also chose to move to South Korea to explore his heritage. His decision both to move there and to search for his family was supported by his adoptive parents. "I understand how parents feel it's a rejection, but I don't feel it at all," his adoptive father, William Hauser, says. "In a sense I'm much closer to him since he's been in Korea."[40] Benjamin reunited with his foster family from his youth but not his biological family. His parents often fly to South Korea to visit him—and together they maintain close family ties.

Do It Again?

Adoptees can never truly know what will happen when they decide to search for their birth parents. Often the result is different than they had envisioned. Mariah Mills grew up knowing that she could request her Minnesota birth certificate at age nineteen to learn who her birth parents were. She longed for this day, wanting to know what they looked like and if she had any biological siblings.

At age nineteen Mills obtained her original birth certificate. From it she learned that her birth father was Tom Burnett, one of the men who helped thwart the hijackers' plans to crash Unit-

Growing Up with Parents and Birth Parents

Some adoptees do not have to search for their birth parents because they have both parents and birth parents in their lives from the time of their adoption. This happens in some open adoptions. Some experts believe this arrangement to be confusing, but many others believe it is positive for adoptees. Juliana Whitney was adopted at birth and has been in contact with her birth parents throughout her life. Most recently, her birth father attended her college graduation. For her an open adoption of this sort was not confusing. It allowed Whitney to understand both her past and present. She grew up understanding that her adoptive parents are her real parents, and her birth parents are people who care about her and love her. She writes:

> [An open adoption] is having the ability to ask your birth parents the questions that adoptees in closed adoptions rarely get answered. It means never wondering if you were given up because your birth parents didn't love you or didn't want you. It means being able to develop a thorough understanding of how and why you wound up somewhere other than in a home with your biological parents.

Juliana Whitney, "What Growing Up in an Open Adoption Has Taught Me as an Adoptee," America Adopts. www .americaadopts.com.

ed Airlines Flight 93 into the White House or Capitol building in Washington, DC, on September 11, 2001. Mills sobbed when she realized her birth father was dead. In the weeks that followed, she tried unsuccessfully to locate her birth mother. Finally, her parents sought the help of a local priest, who knew Burnett's parents. He was able to arrange a meeting between Mills and her biological grandparents and aunt. She also met later with Burnett's widow, Deena, and the couple's daughters—who were Mills's half sisters. Although her biological grandparents did not form a relationship with her, Mills still has a relationship with her biological aunt and with her half sisters and their mother. "I'm now 22 and glad the mystery of where I came from has been

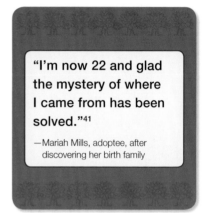

"I'm now 22 and glad the mystery of where I came from has been solved."[41]

—Mariah Mills, adoptee, after discovering her birth family

solved. I have graduated from college and am planning to go to law school," writes Mills. "I love having Deena and my sisters in my life. I'm still coming to grips with the fact that I'll never know Tom. But because of my ongoing relationship with his widow and daughters, I do feel close to him."[41]

As happens with many adoptees, the search for her birth parents had unexpected results. Still, Mills, like many others, believes that it was worth the effort. Finally having answers to her questions about herself has helped her with her life.

Chapter Five

Other People Who Have Families like Mine

Faith Hill is one of country music's most successful performers. Her audiences usually number in the thousands, and fans often sing along with her on songs such as "This Kiss" and "Mississippi Girl." Hill's musical talents are well established: She has five Grammy Awards, six American Music Awards, and fifteen Country Music Awards. She also has a famous husband, country singer Tim McGraw. These are the things Hill is best known for, but she is also known for speaking openly about a topic that is close to her heart: adoption.

Hill was born on September 21, 1967, near Jackson, Mississippi, to twenty-three-year-old Paula Conway. Conway was unmarried at the time and felt that she could not raise her child alone. She decided the best option was adoption. Three days after the baby was born, Ted and Edna Perry adopted her. The Perrys already had two biological sons. They had long prayed to have a daughter, but that had not happened. They gave their new daughter the name Audrey Faith, a name they chose as a testimony to their faith in God.

Childhood Stability

Because Conway made the decision she did, Hill grew up in a stable, happy, loving family. When television talk show host Larry King interviewed Hill in 2006, he asked her about her childhood and implied it had been a tough one because she was adopted. Hill corrected him when she said, "I actually had a pretty amazing childhood. I was adopted, if that's what you're referring to, but my family, my mom and dad and my brothers, they are amazing, very stable, good Christian, God-fearing home, and a great small town of Star, Mississippi. I actually had a really stable childhood."[42]

Hill's aptitude for singing showed up early in her life. At three years old she began singing hymns she had learned at church—using a hairbrush as a microphone. After a while she started singing other kinds of music. She especially liked the songs of Elvis Presley. Her parents encouraged her singing; they even allowed her to attend a Presley concert in 1975 (although they worried somewhat about the influence rock and roll might have on their daughter). This and other childhood experiences laid the groundwork for Hill to follow her dreams of singing.

Adoption Feelings

Hill knew about her adoption from an early age; she grew up with positive feelings about her parents and about being adopted. However, as she grew older, questions and thoughts about her birth parents often came into her mind. She felt a need to learn more. "I was adopted into this incredible home, a loving, positive environment," she recalls, "yet I had this yearning, this kind of darkness that was also inside me."[43]

In 1987, at age nineteen, Hill moved to Nashville to pursue her dream of becoming a country singer. During her first years there, she met Daniel Hill, a songwriter. The couple married, but the marriage did not last. They divorced in 1991, during a period in which Faith was working hard to build her singing career. During this busy and emotional time, Faith continued to think about her birth parents.

> "The first time I met my birth mother, I just stared at her. I'd never seen anyone that looked anything like me."[44]
>
> —Faith Hill

With the help and emotional support of her family, she eventually decided to search for them and finally located her birth mother. Seeing someone biologically related to her felt amazing to Hill. "The first time I met my birth mother, I just stared at her," Hill says. "I'd never seen anyone that looked anything like me. It was the awe of seeing someone you came from. It fills something."[44]

She learned that her birth parents had married years after they gave her up for adoption, and they had a son. Her birth father had died in a car accident while Hill was still young. Hill met her biological brother and continues a relationship with him. Finding her birth family has given Hill answers to her questions about where she came from and what her birth mother was like. Meeting her mother felt like a weight had been lifted from her. It became clear that she had been carrying around the weight of questions about her past. Hill is grateful to her birth mother for making sure her daughter was raised in a loving family. She also credits her adoptive parents for helping shape her into the person she is today.

Country music star Faith Hill, pictured with her husband Tim McGraw, was adopted at birth. She was adopted by what she describes as loving and supportive parents who had prayed for a daughter.

Adopted by Family

Like Hill, Simone Biles credits her parents with providing her with an upbringing that allowed her to follow her dream of being a gymnast. After she was adopted, her parents provided a stable and loving environment in which she thrived. Without their support, she says, she might not have become the three-time gold medal Olympic gymnast that she is today. The first years of Biles's life were tumultuous. She was born on March 14, 1997, in Columbus, Ohio—the third child of four. In the early years of Biles's life, her mother's drug addiction resulted in Biles and her brothers and sisters living in and out of foster homes.

While Biles was in foster care, her mother attended a drug treatment program. The goal was that she would regain custody of her children when she could prove that she had overcome her addiction. That did not happen. Many failed drug tests kept Biles and her siblings in foster care. When Simone was three, she and her sister, Adria, went to live with their grandparents, Ron and Nellie Biles. Simone's two brothers went to live with their great-aunt.

After the girls had been living with their grandparents, whom they called Grandpa and Grandma, Nellie sat the girls down for a talk. "She said, 'It's up to you guys. If you want to, you can call us Mom and Dad,'" Simone remembers. "I went upstairs and tried practicing it in the mirror—'Mom, Dad, Mom, Dad.' Then I went downstairs, and she was in the kitchen. I looked up at her and I was like, 'Mom?' She said, 'Yes!'"[45] The Bileses legally became parents to Simone and her sister when they formally adopted the girls in 2001.

Parents Empowered Her

Simone Biles credits her parents with giving her the encouragement she needed to excel at gymnastics. Her interest in gymnastics began when she was in day care, when the provider took a group of kids to a gymnastics center. The coaches there noted her abilities and contacted her parents to ask that she be allowed to enroll in their classes. Her talent was evident to all. By the time she turned six, her parents had decided to homeschool her so she could focus on gymnastics. She worked hard, and in 2013 she won her first US and world all-around titles. She went on to lead the US Olympic women's gymnastics team during the 2016 Summer Olympic Games.

During the Olympics, Biles dominated the competition. She won three gold medals (in the women's individual all-around, in the vault, and in the floor exercise) and a bronze medal in the balance beam. Between these and her many other World Championship medals, Biles is the most decorated US gymnast ever—with nineteen Olympic and World Championship medals. And there for her throughout all of her years in competition have been her parents, cheering her on and sharing in her success.

"My parents saved me. They've set huge examples of how to treat other people and they've been there to support me since day one."[47]

—Simone Biles

Biles has talked openly about her adoption—and her parents. She has even on occasion corrected those who misunderstand the relationship between adopted children and their parents. During the 2016 Olympics, NBC commentator Al Trautwig introduced Biles to the television audience by saying that she had been raised by her grandfather and his wife and added that she calls them mom and dad. After he said this, Twitter lit up with comments from people who noted that she calls them mom and dad *because they are her mom and dad*. Trautwig responded by tweeting that her adoptive parents were not her real parents. At this point, Biles entered the fray with her own response. She tweeted, "My parents are my parents and that's it."[46]

Since the Olympics, Biles has published an autobiography, *Courage to Soar*, appeared on the show *Dancing with the Stars*, and is preparing for the 2020 Olympics. While on *Dancing with the Stars*, she dedicated her dance to her parents so they would know what they mean to her. "My parents saved me. They've set

Famous Adoptive Parents

Angelina Jolie and Brad Pitt, Sandra Bullock, Meg Ryan, and Madonna are just some of the many celebrities who have embraced adoption. Adoption advocates believe that their actions have cast a positive light on adoption and helped others realize that adoption is just another way to become a family. Celebrities' reasons for adopting are as varied as those of other people. Actress Sandra Bullock was thinking about all of the children in need of families when she decided to adopt Louis, a baby, in 2010 and Laila, a three-and-a-half-year-old, from foster care in 2015. "When I look at Laila, there's no doubt in my mind that she was supposed to be here. I can tell you absolutely, the exact right children came to me at the exact right time," she says. For Bullock and other celebrities who are adoptive parents, adoption was a normal way to become a family.

Quoted in *People*, "Sandra Bullock Is a Mom Again! Meet Her Adorable Daughter, Laila," December 2, 2015. http://celebritybabies.people.com.

huge examples of how to treat other people and they've been there to support me since day one," Biles says. "There's nothing I could say to them to thank them enough."[47]

Differences and Strength

Another athlete, Colin Kaepernick, is best known for his athletic abilities as a professional football player and for his game-day protests against racial injustice. Kaepernick needed both physical and mental strength for these endeavors. The former San Francisco 49ers quarterback says he learned to treat others with respect and other life lessons from his parents, who adopted him when he was an infant. He has also learned these lessons from his experiences as a child of an interracial adoption.

Colin Kaepernick was born on November 3, 1987, in Milwaukee, Wisconsin. His biological mother was nineteen and Caucasian.

At three years old, US Olympic gymnast Simone Biles was legally adopted by her grandparents. Biles credits them with giving her the support she needed to excel at gymnastics.

His biological father, an African American, was not in the picture. Young and alone, his mother decided to give her baby up for adoption. A Caucasian couple, Rick and Teresa Kaepernick, adopted the baby a few weeks after his birth. The Kaepernicks already had two biological children, and they had lost two other babies due to birth defects.

Throughout Colin's childhood, the Kaepernicks openly discussed both adoption and their different races. "We've always been really open about the adoption, and we were always very open about the skin colors," Teresa told the *New York Times* in 2010. "We pointed it out as a positive, and he saw his difference and was comfortable with it."[48]

Although Kaepernick's family focused on the positives of his adoption and race, and he was proud of both, he still dealt with outside negativity. Less than 2 percent of people in Turlock, California, where his family moved when he was four, were black. He learned early on that others would treat him differently because of his skin color and his adoption. For one, classmates would tell him his parents could not really be his parents, since they were a different race. As he got older, he noticed other oddities in people's behavior toward him. "We used to go on these summer driving vacations and stay at motels," Kaepernick says. "And every year, in the lobby of every motel, the same thing always happened, and it only got worse as I got older and taller. It didn't matter how close I stood to my family, somebody would walk up to me, a real nervous manager, and say: 'Excuse me. Is there something I can help you with?'"[49] Only when they realized he was with his Caucasian parents did the people working at the motels leave him alone.

Rising to Strength

Dealing with racial prejudice and adoption questions did not keep Kaepernick from developing as a student and an athlete. As he grew older, he excelled at both. He played youth football in California at age eight, and the coach placed him in the quarterback position due to his strong arm. In 2007 he enrolled at the University of Nevada–Reno after he was recruited to play safety on the school's football team. During the fifth game of the year, Kaepernick played quarterback after the team's starter was injured. He remained in this position throughout college, setting several records.

After Kaepernick graduated from college, the San Francisco 49ers selected him in the second round of the 2011 National Football League draft. He played as a 49er on and off as starting quarterback until the spring of 2017. He then opted out of his contract with the 49ers to become a free agent but was not signed to a team in 2017.

Social Views Influenced

Kaepernick's adoption, race, and family upbringing have influenced his efforts to pursue justice for and inspire others. "I want

Adopted and Adopting

In addition to being a celebrity who was adopted, gold medal Olympic ice skater Scott Hamilton also has adopted his own children. Hamilton was adopted in 1958 at six weeks old. His parents sacrificed much in order for Hamilton to pursue ice skating, and they supported him in all he did. His experiences as an adoptee led him on the path to adopting his children. He and his wife, Tracie, had two biological children; then in 2014 they adopted Evelyne, eleven, and Jean Paul, thirteen, both from Haiti. After a major earthquake struck Haiti in 2010, Tracie traveled to Haiti to help and connected with Live Beyond, an organization that partners with an orphanage in the village of Thomazeau. They saw a picture of Jean Paul, then Tracie went to meet him and his little sister, Evelyne. "We fell in love with these kids two years ago and it took us that long to bring them home," Hamilton said in 2014. "They're beautiful, beautiful children and our hearts are twice the size they were before. We're blessed beyond our wildest dreams."

Quoted in A. Pawlowski, "Scott Hamilton Opens Up About Adopting Two Kids from Haiti," *Today*, November 21, 2014. www.today.com.

to have a positive influence as much as I can," Kaepernick says. "I've had people write me because of my tattoos. I've had people write me because of adoption. I've had people write me because they're biracial. So, to me, the more people you can touch, the more people you can influence in a positive way or inspire, the better."[50]

One of the ways he decided to influence others was to kneel during the national anthem before a game in 2016. He knelt to protest racial injustice, especially the police shootings of young, unarmed African American men. This protest angered many people, who felt his actions were anti-American. But others, including many pro football players and team owners, began engaging in their own game-day protests.

Throughout this period of controversy, Kaepernick's parents voiced support for their son's efforts. Teresa and Rick Kaepernick wrote in a 2016 statement:

> Colin is carrying a heavy load and following a difficult path that he truly believes in. He is putting his entire future and possibly his life on the line for those beliefs. As his parents, it pains us to read articles and tweets saying that his family does not support him; this could not be further from the truth. We want people to know that we are very proud of our son and admire his strength and courage in kneeling for the rights of others.[51]

Life Relationships

Kaepernick has spoken publicly about the influence his parents have had on him and how they have been integral in forming his character. He has remained close to them and includes them in much of his life.

"It's just—that's my family. That's it."[52]

—Collin Kaepernick

Although he has known who his birth mother is for years, Kaepernick has chosen not to develop a relationship with her. He is not alone. Many people who are adopted see no need to reconnect with their birth parents. "It's not really a respect thing," he said when asked if he did not want to meet his birth mother out of respect for his parents. "It's just—that's my family. That's it."[52]

Experiences of adoption differ from one person to the next. This can be seen in the experiences of Faith Hill, Simone Biles, and Colin Kaepernick. Like all adoptees, their experiences and feelings about adoption are unique. Likewise, their adoptions have helped shape who they are.

Source Notes

Chapter One: How American Families Are Changing

1. Curtis Rogers, "Where Did You Get the Idea You Could Raise a Black Child?," *Chicago Now* (blog), November, 2013. www.chicagonow.com.
2. Rogers, "Where Did You Get the Idea You Could Raise a Black Child?"
3. Rogers, "Where Did You Get the Idea You Could Raise a Black Child?"
4. Pew Research Center, "Parenting in America," December 17, 2015. www.pewsocialtrends.org.
5. Caitlin, "Ask Me Anything, We're a Transracial Family," *Real Mom Recs* (blog), 2017. www.realmomrecs.com.
6. Quoted in Amanda Hengel, "Foreign Territory," *South Jersey Magazine*, November 2013. http://southjerseymagazine.com.
7. Quoted in *Huffington Post*, "Children of LGBT Parents Speak Out for the Let Love Define Family Series," December 12, 2014. www.huffingtonpost.com.
8. Quoted in Kate Hakala, "Meet the Single, Twenty Something Women Who Are Trying to Adopt Kids," Mic, 2017. https://mic.com.
9. Jillian Lauren, "A Letter to Jovi Starshine on His Gotcha Day," *Jillian Lauren Blog*, December 19, 2016. www.jillianlauren.com.
10. Rachel Garlinghouse, "We're a Real Family, Thank You Very Much," American SPCC, November 18, 2017. https://americanspcc.org.

Chapter Two: How I See Myself and My Family

11. Lisa Cleary, "6 Things My Adoptive Parents Did Right," *Today*, November 25, 2014. www.today.com.
12. Quoted in Chris Bodenner, "When Adoption Turns to Agony," *Atlantic*, September 2016. www.theatlantic.com.
13. Judy Myerson and Sara Myerson, "What We Wish We Had Known," CCAI, May 12, 2016. www.ccaifamily.org.

14. Leslie Tousley, "The Story of an Adult Adoptee," Adoption .com, 2018. https://adoption.com.
15. Maria Williams, "How Does It Feel to Be Adopted?," How Does It Feel to Be Adopted?, November 18, 2016. https:// howdoesitfeeltobeadopted.com.
16. Mae Claire, "How Does It Feel to Be Adopted?," How Does It Feel to Be Adopted?, November 7, 2015. https://howdoesit feeltobeadopted.com.
17. Emma Goddard, "I Hate Being Judged Because I Look Different from My Adoptive Family," *Good Housekeeping*, December 14, 2015. www.goodhousekeeping.com.
18. Quoted in Don Aucoin, "The Roots of the Problem," Boston. com, March 31, 2009. http://archive.boston.com.
19. Pamela Karanova, "Grief & Loss & Adoption," Adoptee in Recovery, September 23, 2015. https://adopteeinrecovery.com.
20. Gerald Wozek, "My Birthmark: Finding My Real Family," Pieces of Me: Who Do I Want to Be?, 2009. www.emkpress.com.
21. Kelley Marie, "How Does It Feel to Be Adopted?," How Does It Feel to Be Adopted?, November 6, 2016. https://howdoesit feeltobeadopted.com.

Chapter Three: How the World Sees Me and My Family

22. Kristen Howerton, "Parents, Please Educate Your Kids About Adoption So Mine Don't Have To," *Huffington Post*, December 6, 2017. www.huffpost.com.
23. Dot Saiz, "8 Things Adopted People Are Tired of Hearing," Thought Catalog, August 14, 2017. www.thoughtcatalog.com.
24. Julie Fraga, "Just Because I'm Adopted Doesn't Mean I Have to Answer All Your Questions," *Good Housekeeping*, December 11, 2015. www.goodhousekeeping.com.
25. Goddard, "I Hate Being Judged Because I Look Different from My Adoptive Family."
26. Quoted in *Weekend Edition Sunday*, "Growing Up 'White,' Transracial Adoptee Learned to Be Black," NPR, July 26, 2014. www.npr.org.
27. Quoted in WNYC, "Growing Up with Gay Parents," May 25, 2015. www.wnyc.org.

28. Michelle, "True Story: I Went Through Foster Care," Yes and Yes, August 2010. www.yesandyes.org.
29. Quoted in Abbie Goldberg, "Stigmas About Adoption Remain and Hurt Families," *Beyond Blood* (blog), *Psychology Today*, May 21, 2012. www.psychologytoday.com.
30. Carrie Goldman, "The 'Real Parents' Question to Stop Asking Adopted Kids," *Huffington Post*, January 12, 2013. www.huffingtonpost.com.
31. Mei Webb, "Stop Telling Me I'm 'So Lucky,'" *The Blog*, *Huffington Post*, May 20, 2016. www.huffingtonpost.com.

Chapter Four: Searching for Birth Parents

32. Quoted in Elizabeth Durand Streisand, "After Searching for 30 Years, I Finally Found My Birth Mother," *Good Housekeeping*, December 22, 2015. www.goodhousekeeping.com.
33. Quoted in Kate Hilpern, "Adoption Reunions, There Is No Doubt That the Road Gets Bumpy," *Guardian* (Manchester), December 29, 2012. www.theguardian.com.
34. Quoted in Stephanie Booth, "I Went Looking for My Birth Parents and Realized My Father Was Famous," *Cosmopolitan*, November 25, 2015. www.cosmopolitan.com.
35. Rosie Garland, "Why I Have Never Felt the Need to Find My Birth Mother," *Telegraph* (London), August 10, 2014. www.telegraph.co.uk.
36. Stephen Betchen, "Why Adoptees Need to Find Their Biological Parents," *Magnetic Partners* (blog), *Psychology Today*, August 3, 2011. www.psychologytoday.com.
37. Maggie Geimer, "It Happened to Me: I Found My Birthmother and She Didn't Want to Meet Me," *xoJane*, November 4, 2015. www.xojane.com.
38. Kimberly Eddy, "Looking for My Birth Mother," Boundless, January 15, 2009. www.boundless.org.
39. Eddy, "Looking for My Birth Mother."
40. Quoted in Maggie Jones, "Why a Generation of Adoptees Is Returning to South Korea," *New York Times*, January 1, 2015. www.nytimes.com.
41. Quoted in Booth, "I Went Looking for My Birth Parents and Realized My Father Was Famous."

Chapter Five: Other People
Who Have Families like Mine

42. Quoted in Fox News, "Faith Hill's Mother Dead at 80," November 1, 2016. www.foxnews.com.

43. Quoted in Leah Ginsburg, "How Faith Hill Found Happiness," *Good Housekeeping*, April 2004. www.goodhousekeeping.com.

44. Quoted in Ginsburg, "How Faith Hill Found Happiness."

45. Quoted in Rachel Larimore, "Why Does NBC's Al Trautwig Refuse to Call Simone Biles' Adoptive Parents Her Parents?," *Five Ring Circus* (blog), *Slate*, August 8, 2016. www.slate.com.

46. Quoted in Angela Fritz, "Do You Know Who Your Real Parents Are?," *Washington Post*, August 12, 2016. www.washingtonpost.com.

47. Quoted in Char Adams, "Simone Biles Breaks Down While Talking About the Year She Was Adopted: 'My Parents Saved Me,'" *People*, April 10, 2017. http://people.com.

48. Quoted in Adam Himmelsbach, "Not a Household Name, Not Even in Nevada," *New York Times*, August 29, 2010. www.nytimes.com.

49. Quoted in John Branch, "The Awakening of Colin Kaepernick," *New York Times*, September 7, 2017. www.nytimes.com.

50. Quoted in Peter King, "Colin Kaepernick Does Not Care What You Think About His Tattoos," *Sports Illustrated*, July 23, 2013. www.si.com.

51. Quoted in Martenzie Johnson, "Colin Kaepernick's Parents Break Silence: 'We Absolutely Do Support Him,'" ESPN, December 10, 2016. www.espn.com.

52. Quoted in Rebecca Carroll, "Why It's Perfectly Acceptable That Colin Kaepernick Doesn't Want to Meet His Birthmother," *Good*, February 5, 2013. www.good.is.

For Further Research

Books

Chris Beam, *To the End of June: The Intimate Life of American Foster Care*. Wilmington, MA: Mariner, 2014.

Simone Biles, *Courage to Soar: A Body in Motion, a Life in Balance*. Grand Rapids, MI: Zondervan, 2016.

Rebecca Compton, *Adoption Beyond Borders: How International Adoption Benefits Children*. Oxford: Oxford University Press, 2016.

Glen Lukemba, *Adopted by White Parents*. Seattle: Amazon Digital Services, 2015.

Caitriona Palmer, *Affair with My Mother*. London: Penguin, 2017.

Internet Sources

Eliza Carney, "Understanding Open Adoption Pros and Cons," *Adoptive Families*, May 28, 2016. www.adoptivefamilies.com /openness/understanding-open-adoption.

Amy Guimond, "I Was Adopted as a Child, but That Doesn't Define Who I Am," *Huffington Post*, January 10, 2013. www.huff ingtonpost.com/2013/01/10/how-being-adopted-as-a-child -affects-me_n_2447477.html.

Leslie Mann, "What to Expect When You Find Your Birth Parents," *Chicago Tribune*, March 11, 2016. www.chicagotribune. com/lifestyles/sc-finding-birth-parents-family-0315-20160311 -story.html.

Stephanie, "I'm Adopted and This Is the One Thing I Wish People Would Stop Saying," MTV, November 2, 2015. www.mtv.com /news/2367294/im-adopted-and-this-is-the-one-thing-i-wish -people-would-stop-saying.

Karen Valby, "The Realities of Raising a Kid of a Different Race," *Time*, 2017. http://time.com/the-realities-of-raising-a-kid-of-a -different-race.

Organizations and Websites

Adoptive Families (www.adoptivefamlies.org). This online resource for information about adopting offers guidance and help for adopted families. It provides articles on issues such as adoption awareness at school, raising children of different races, and other adoption-related issues.

AdoptUSKids (www.adoptuskids.org). AdoptUSKids is a project of the US Children's Bureau, and its mission is to help child welfare systems connect children in foster care with adoptive families. It provides information on how to adopt from foster care, includes foster care adoption stories, and highlights children on the list for adoption.

National Adoption Center (www.adopt.org). This website provides information about adoption in the United States, including personal stories of adoption. It also includes articles and information specific to families considering adoption, foster care adoption, and adoptees considering searching for birth parents.

Index

Picture Credits